PEARY REACHES THE NORTH POLE

Gordon Charleston

Dillon Press
New York

First American publication 1993 by Dillon Press,
Macmillan Publishing Company,
866 Third Avenue, New York, NY 10022

Macmillan Publishing Company is part of the
Maxwell Communication Group of Companies.

First published in Great Britain by Zoë Books
Limited

A ZOË BOOK

Devised and produced by
Zoë Books Limited
15 Worthy Lane
Winchester
Hampshire SO23 7AB
England

Printed in Italy by Grafedit SpA
Design: Jan Sterling, Sterling Associates
Picture research: Faith Perkins
Illustrations and maps: Gecko Limited
Production: Grahame Griffiths

10 9 8 7 6 5 4 3 2 1

Library of Congress Cataloging-in-Publication Data

Charleston, Gordon.
  Peary reaches the North Pole / Gordon
    Charleston. p. cm — (Great 20th century
    expeditions)
  Includes bibliographical references.
  Summary: Describes Admiral Peary's attempts
to reach the North Pole in the early twentieth
century and the dispute of his claim to have been
the first succeed.
  ISBN 0-87518-535-5
  1. Peary, Robert E. (Robert Edwin), 1856-1920
— Juvenile literature. 2. Explorers — United
States — Biography — Juvenile literature. 3.
North Pole. [1. Peary. Robert E. (Robert Edwin),
1856-1920. 2. Explorers. 3. North Pole.] I. Title.
II. Series.
G635.P4C43 1993
919.804'092 — dc20
[B]   92-44500

Photographic acknowledgments

The publishers wish to acknowledge, with thanks,
the following photographic sources:
Bryan & Cherry Alexander: title, 5t, 5b, 9, 13b,
17b, 19, 26, 28; The Bridgeman Art Library: 8t
(National Maritime Museum); R. K. Headland,
Scott Polar Research Institute, Cambridge: 27b, 29;
Michael Holford: 7b; Hulton-Deutsch Collection:
10t, 14, 15t, 21 (Bettman Archive), 22, 23t, 23b,
24, 25b; By courtesy of the National Portrait
Gallery, London: 7t; The Royal Geographical
Society: 11, 12, 17t, 20t; Syndication
International: 13t; The Tate Gallery, London: 6;
Topham Picture Source: 8b, 18b, 20b, 25t, 27t.

Cover Photographs: courtesy of Bryan & Cherry
Alexander and The Royal Geographical Society

The publishers have made every effort to trace the
copyright holders, but if they have inadvertently
overlooked any, they will be pleased to make the
necessary arrangement at the first opportunity.

Contents

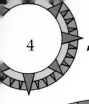

The "top of the world"

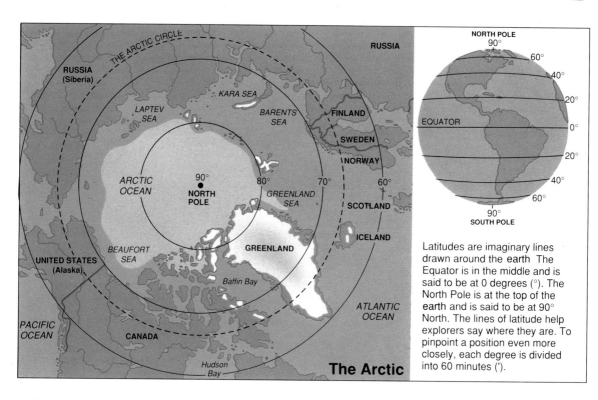

The Arctic

Latitudes are imaginary lines drawn around the earth The Equator is in the middle and is said to be at 0 degrees (°). The North Pole is at the top of the earth and is said to be at 90° North. The lines of latitude help explorers say where they are. To pinpoint a position even more closely, each degree is divided into 60 minutes (').

What is the North Pole? Where is it, and why have so many explorers wanted to find it? If you look at a map of the world, or a **globe**, you will see that north points toward the top. The North Pole is the name of the place that is the farthest north that anyone can go. It is the "top of the world."

First at the top

At 10 o'clock on the morning of April 6, 1909, Robert E. Peary of the U. S. Navy stood with his team of explorers at the top of the world. Peary had spent more than 20 years trying to reach the North Pole. This was his third attempt, and now he and his team of explorers and dogs had arrived. They were the first to reach that place, which other explorers had tried

and failed to find. For Peary, it was the moment that he had dreamed of all his life.

An ice desert

Peary and his team were standing on a frozen ocean. All around them, as far as they could see, was ice. The ocean stretched to the horizon, sometimes in mounds or ridges, but mostly there was a flat, endless view of ice. The North Pole is in the middle of the Arctic Ocean, which is frozen solid for most of the year. It is one of the coldest places on earth.

Very few animals go out onto the ice, because there is less chance of finding food there than on land. Polar bears and arctic foxes have sometimes been seen in spring or summer. At that time of year the

▲ Icebergs and frozen sea, in the Arctic

ice breaks up and the animals search for fish, seal, or **walrus**. No plants grow, and no birds live on the ice. It is an ice desert.

The people of the north

The Inuit people live nearest to the North Pole, several hundred miles to the south. For hundreds of years they have lived by hunting animals and fishing in the sea. Many explorers have copied the Inuit style of dress, their homes, and their way of traveling in order to try to stay alive in the bitter cold of the Arctic. Peary learned about how to survive from Inuit people, and many of his team members were Inuit.

Why go to the Pole?

For some explorers it may be the excitement of being the first to do something that makes them want to explore. In the past many people hoped to find lands that were new to them, where there might be gold or silver, and where they might become rich. Other explorers looked for new routes to travel to other countries. They wanted to buy and sell goods, and the routes they discovered are called trade routes.

Trade routes

About 500 years ago the North Pole became important to traders and sailors. The trade routes between Europe and the Far East, particularly China, were fiercely guarded by the Spanish and the Portuguese. Sailors from other trading nations such as Britain and Holland were attacked if they tried to sail south to the Far East around the tip of Africa. They knew of the route around South America, but it was long and dangerous. People thought there might be a shorter, northern route. However, the first explorers could go no farther than the Arctic ice.

▼ Polar bears live only in the Arctic.

Early explorers

Henry Hudson

Many of the first people who tried to find a trade route between the Atlantic Ocean and the Pacific Ocean were British. Among the first of these **navigators** was Henry Hudson. In 1607 he sailed north until his ship was blocked by ice near Spitsbergen. He then headed westward, around the edge of the ice. This expedition was paid for by a group of traders, or **merchants**, who hoped to use the new route to send goods to and from the Far East. Hudson did not open up a new way to China, but in the far north he found that there were fish, whales, seals, foxes, and bears. The Hudson's Bay Company soon began to trade in fish and furs.

▼ In 1611 there was a mutiny on board Henry Hudson's boat. The crew left Hudson, his son, and another sailor to drift in the icy seas.

Phipps and Lutwidge

In 1773 the Royal Society, based in London, suggested to the Royal Navy that a polar route to the Pacific might be possible. Captains Constantine Phipps and Lutwidge were chosen to lead this attempt. Their ships were also stopped by ice, just north of Spitsbergen. They were unable to move, and the crews had to leave in smaller boats. However, Captain Lutwidge noticed that the surface of the ice was smooth and firm, and he suggested that the route to the Pole might be successful if people traveled over the ice, rather than trying to sail north.

Parry's attempts

About 50 years later another Royal Navy officer, William Edward Parry, read Lutwidge's notes. Parry had commanded three Arctic expeditions, the first in 1819, looking for a Northwest Passage. Parry was convinced that land travel would succeed. He persuaded the Royal Navy to arrange another expedition. This time he aimed to reach the North Pole.

Parry ordered special boats from the naval dockyards. They were flat-bottomed, and very light. These boats had metal-covered runners on the bottom, so that they could be pulled over the ice.

Parry's expedition to the Pole set off in April 1827, reaching Spitsbergen a month later. The special boats were lowered onto the ice, but they were too heavy to move very far, even with 14 men pulling each one. Parry found that the ice was not as

▲ William Edward Parry

smooth as he hoped — and it rained. The rain made the ice form sharp, jagged edges. It was sharp enough to cut their boots. Finally Parry's scientific measurements showed that they were in fact traveling south, not north! The **pack ice** was slowly moving south, and they were not traveling fast enough to make any progress north.

After this, the British put their energy into finding a Northwest Passage.

▼ Two of the ships in Parry's 1825 expedition

The American Way

▲ Sir John Franklin

British attempts to find the Northwest Passage aroused a great deal of interest in North America. The Americans, too, sent expeditions to find the northern Atlantic-Pacific route. They also wanted to find out what had happened to Sir John Franklin, a British explorer who had been missing since 1845 while he was attempting to find the passage.

Elisha Kent Kane

In 1853 an American expedition, led by Elisha Kent Kane, sailed up the coast of Greenland to Rensselaer Harbor. This was the farthest point that any ship had sailed in winter. Kane set up **search parties**, equipped with **sledges** pulled by dogs. Kane learned to dress and travel as the Inuit people did, which helped his teams to survive and also to travel faster over the ice. Kane did not find Franklin, and he did not reach the Pole, but he had explored about a third of the route that came to be called the American Way to the Pole. He had also learned a great deal about polar travel, clothing, and survival, which was of use to other explorers.

Hall's expedition

Another American, Charles Francis Hall, set out to find Franklin. Hall was helped by the United States government. His ship, the *Polaris*, was a U.S. Navy tug. By August 30, 1871, the ship had reached 82°14' north, only 34 miles (54 kilometers) south of Parry's record. However, **blizzards** and strong currents drove the ship south again, to the coast of Greenland and the expedition returned to the United States.

Although neither Kane nor Hall managed to go as far north as Parry, they had between them charted the American Way between Smith Sound and the

▼ Charles Francis Hall's polar expedition

▲ In the summer part of the pack ice breaks up into large blocks of ice that drift in the sea.

Atlantic Ocean. Later this came to be the best route from which to approach the North Pole.

World interest

Kane's and Hall's attempts inspired many younger Americans to explore the far north, among them Robert E. Peary. People in other countries heard about their progress, too, and began to send teams of their own to the Arctic.

An Austrian expedition in 1872-1874 found a new land, which the explorers named Franz Josef Land after their emperor. In 1875 the British sent a Royal Navy team, led by Captain George Nares, whose aim was to reach the North Pole. Nares sailed northwest along the coast of Ellesmere Island, and sent out sledge teams led by Lieutenant Albert Markham. For the first time, the teams went on to pack ice. They broke Parry's record and reached 83°20' north before they had to turn back.

Breaking records

Between 1883 and 1900 two further attempts made progress toward the Pole. The Norwegian Fridtjof Nansen, supported by the Norwegian king, Parliament, and wealthy people, had the idea of sailing a ship into the Arctic ice and letting it drift across to the Pole. It did drift, but very slowly. After 19 months Nansen and another man, Hjalmar Johansen, set out across the ice by sledge. They reached 86°14' north before turning back three weeks later. They were stopped by ridge upon ridge of ice.

Five years later an Italian team led by the Duke of the Abruzzi set out for the Pole. Commander Umberto Cagni of the Italian Navy sledged to 86°34' north — a new record. This proved that conditions in the Arctic Ocean were different from year to year.

The next person to make an attempt on the North Pole was Robert E. Peary.

Peary's first attempts

▲ Peary in his naval uniform

Robert E. Peary had watched with interest the steady progress of other expeditions toward the North Pole. Peary was a civil engineer in the U.S. Navy. He had risen to become a commander, and had led expeditions into Greenland to make maps of its coastline. He also dug up **meteorites** to take back to American museums.

The first journey

After 16 years in Greenland, Peary decided it was time to try for the Pole. On April 6, 1902, Peary, his comrade Matthew Henson, and four Inuit set out. They left the land in the far north of Ellesmere Island, and began to sledge across the Arctic ice. After 15 days they had to turn back. Conditions were dreadful. The team was forced to zigzag across the ice to avoid ridges, rough ice, and cracks called **leads** that opened up

in the ice. They had to hack out a **trail** with **ice axes**, in biting wind and blinding snow and ice storms. It was minus 60°F (minus 51°C). They could not go on, and they had broken no records. They were at 84°16' north.

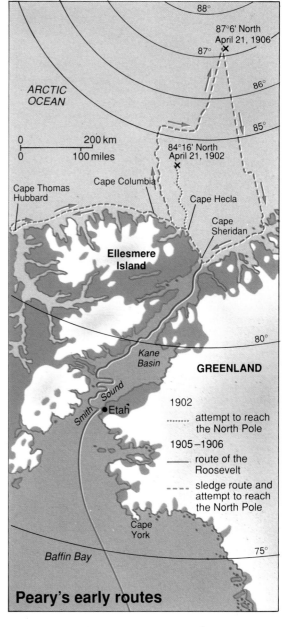

Peary's early routes

The second attempt

Three years later Peary tried again. This time he reached 87°6' north, a new record. Peary now knew that his methods were correct. The only thing that prevented him from going on was a huge lead that opened up in the ice, delaying the team while they waited for it to close again. When it did, their provisions were low, and when a blizzard came, they had to turn back. In New York, Peary was given a hero's welcome. He was determined to try again. Peary's problem, as usual, was lack of money.

Raising money

Polar expeditions cost a great deal of money. Peary had leave of absence from the navy, which meant that he was on half pay. At this time he had no government backing.

A group of business people, bankers, and wealthy **tycoons** set up the Peary Arctic Club to help Peary to pay for his explorations. Some of these people owned museums and were interested in what Peary might find in his travels. Other members of the club wanted to help Peary to reach the North Pole because they shared his dream. Peary did raise money by giving lectures and by writing about his work, and he was also helped by the National Geographic Society. The Arctic Club provided the money to repair Peary's ship and to buy supplies for the new expedition.

▶ Peary's ship, the *Roosevelt*

The *Roosevelt*

Peary's ship was named after President Theodore Roosevelt. It was built for the 1905-1906 trip and was a steamship with sails. The ship was short and strongly built with steel plating to prevent it from being crushed by ice. On deck were three railroad cars that provided sleeping rooms for the crew. The ship's propeller and rudder could be lifted clear of pack ice. The ship's sides were egg-shaped so that it would rise when it was squeezed by the pack ice. The sides were up to 30 inches (76 centimeters) thick.

In spite of all these special features, the *Roosevelt* was badly damaged. By the time the repairs were finished Peary had been delayed by a year. However, in 1908 he was ready to set out on his next attempt to reach the North Pole.

▲ Robert E. Peary in his North Pole "costume"

Preparing for the journey

Peary had spent more than 16 years as an explorer in the Arctic before he began to try to reach the North Pole. He learned from the Inuit people how to survive — and how to travel safely — in the polar desert.

Peary built his own sledge in the style of an Inuit sledge. Its base was high off the ground, so that the uneven surface of the ice would not scrape it. He found that strips of steel could be used as sledge runners so that the sledge would cut through the ice. His **dog harness** was made from canvas, and the **traces** were linen. Polar explorers knew from experience that the dogs would eat the traces if they were made from walrus skin. Peary also improved the way a paraffin stove burned, so that it would boil 1 gallon (4 liters) of icy water in five minutes.

How to stay alive

Like the Inuit, Peary and his team dressed in fox furs and sealskins. They also used reindeer **hide** and bearskins for clothing, which kept out the wind and did not absorb moisture. Anything wet would freeze solid. Peary did not use tents, which could also freeze. His team slept in the open, sheltering behind their sledges and covered by furs. When the cold became too severe, they built ice houses, or **igloos**. The Inuit had taught Peary how to build igloos, how to drive a dog sledge, and how to make clothes out of furs.

What to eat

For food, the team took blocks of dried beef, called **pemmican**. The beef was ground into powder, then mixed with animal fat and turned into blocks. Sometimes raisins or chocolate were added. Most polar explorers ate pemmican, as they still do today.

Watching the weight!

Peary wanted to travel as lightly as possible. Any heavy equipment or supplies

▲ Dogs and men had to work together to pull the sledges over a ridge such as this one. These ridges of ice and snow are formed by movements of the ice.

would weigh down the sledges. This would make it more difficult for the dogs to pull the sledges over the rough ice, and progress would be slower.

Peary decided to take as few team members as he could. He said that they should be "small, wiry men." Small men would eat less of the food and would not take up too much room in the igloos!

▶ An igloo provides shelter from the freezing polar winds. Igloos are built from blocks of ice, in the shape of a dome.

Peary's team

Peary planned to cross the Arctic Ocean as he did in 1906, with six sledge teams. He called these teams divisions. Three of the divisions were headed by Peary's old friends. Captain Bob Bartlett was the master of Peary's ship, the *Roosevelt*. Bartlett came from Newfoundland and was thirty years old. He was a pipe smoker, and Peary even allowed him to bring along tobacco, which added to the weight of the supplies! Ross Marvin was Peary's secretary. He was a professor at Cornell University and was also an engineer. He had been with Peary on the 1906 expedition.

Matthew Henson was an old friend and companion of Peary. He had been Peary's assistant for more than 20 years. Henson was admired by the Inuit people for his skills at hunting and at sledge driving. He could also speak their language very well.

▼ Matthew Henson, the American explorer, went on seven Arctic expeditions with Peary.

▲ Dr. John Goodsell

New leaders

The other three division leaders were newcomers. Dr. John Goodsell came from New Kensington, Pennsylvania. He was the expedition's doctor. Donald Macmillan was a schoolmaster from Worcester Academy, Massachusetts, and George Borup had recently finished studying at Yale University.

Among them the division leaders had many different skills and interests. However, they all believed in one thing. They shared Peary's dream of being part of the expedition that would reach the North Pole first.

The team members included twenty-two Inuit, and the sledges were pulled by teams of dogs. Peary took more than 200 dogs on the expedition, together with 118 tons of whale and walrus meat to feed them. It was necessary to take such a large number of dogs because many would die

on the journey. Peary knew from experience that most of the dogs would die of exhaustion or disease.

Peary's determination to succeed

Peary was more determined than ever that this attempt to reach the Pole should succeed. Since his childhood he had dreamed of the North Pole. Now his ambition to be the first person at the Pole drove him on. Peary could be a difficult man. He quarreled with other polar explorers when he thought they were using routes that "belonged" to him. He would allow nothing and no one to stop him. Even though he had lost all but one toe on each foot through **frostbite**, he carried on. This time he would succeed.

▼ Peary would have used a **sextant** like this to find his way to the North Pole. He would have looked through the telescope and then used the mirrors to measure the angle between the sun and the horizon. With the help of a compass and a watch he could work out exactly where he was.

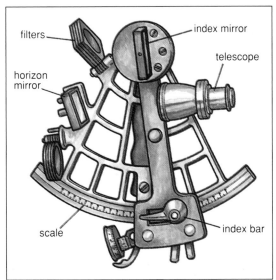

To the North Pole

Sailing north

The *Roosevelt* sailed from New York on July 6, 1908, heading for Greenland. More than one month later, on August 18, the ship left Etah. The team members left behind a large quantity of supplies at Etah for their return journey. Now the ship also carried the Inuit team members, including some of their wives, together with the dogs and food for the dogs. About twenty days later

the ship lay at anchor at Cape Sheridan. It had pushed its way through the ice-strewn sea. There the team set up another **depot** and made ready their equipment. New team members were introduced and had the chance to get used to the weather conditions of the far north. At this point Peary began to take careful measurements and notes of the tides and winds. These records were very important later on.

From ship to sledge

One by one the sledge divisions set out for Cape Columbia, which was 90 miles (144 kilometers) away. This was the last land before the pack ice of the Arctic Ocean. At Cape Columbia they set up Camp Crane. The North Pole lay 413 miles (660 kilometers) away, in the desert of jumbled ice.

By now it was getting close to the Arctic winter, and there would be no more daylight for many months. Peary hoped for moonlight so that he could send his teams ahead to set up depots of supplies and to hunt for food. During the months they spent at Camp Crane, the members of the expedition had more time to get used to the bitter weather. They even lived in the open air, wearing their clothing made of animal fur.

Over the frozen ocean

Peary planned to start moving north across the ice at the end of February 1909. By that time everything was ready at Camp Crane. It was bitterly cold, minus

route of the Roosevelt
sledge route

0   600 km
0   300 miles

ARCTIC OCEAN

Cape Columbia (Camp Crane)
Cape Sheridan

Queen Elizabeth Islands

Ellesmere Island

Kane Basin
Etah

GREENLAND

Baffin Bay

Baffin Island

Davis Strait

Hudson Strait

Hudson Bay

Labrador

ATLANTIC OCEAN

CANADA

Ottawa

Gulf of St Lawrence   Newfoundland

UNITED STATES

New York

From New York to Camp Crane

◀ Captain Bob Bartlett (*far right*) with his sledge division. The Inuit Ooqueah is sitting next to Bartlett.

58°F (minus 50°C), but the snow base was rock hard, which was exactly what Peary wanted.

On February 28 the first two divisions, led by Bartlett and Borup, set out. Peary, with the other four divisions, was to follow the next day. Almost at once Bartlett and Borup were held up by an open crack in the ice. This lead took twenty-four hours to close up before the two teams could continue north. That day, March 1, Peary awoke to a fierce east wind and a gray haze over the ice field. He had never known such conditions — even the Inuit were dismayed. Not only would the wind open up leads of water in the ice, it would also be very hard on the teams. It would blow stinging ice and snow against them — hard enough to draw blood. In spite of this, Peary gave the order to start the journey. Twenty-four men, 19 sledges, and 133 dogs charged along the ice under a ferocious wind, in the bitter cold of minus 50°F (minus 45°C).

▼ Leads like this one delayed Peary's team. In this picture Inuit people are fishing in the lead.

Day by day

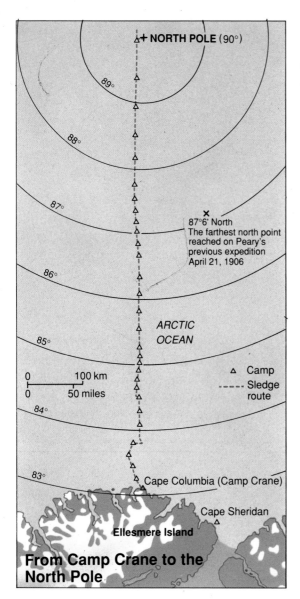

∆+ NORTH POLE (90°)

89°

88°

87°

×
87°6' North
The farthest north point
reached on Peary's
previous expedition
April 21, 1906

86°

*ARCTIC
OCEAN*

85°

0	100 km
0	50 miles

∆ Camp
----- Sledge
route

84°

83° ∆ Cape Columbia (Camp Crane)

Cape Sheridan
∆

Ellesmere Island

**From Camp Crane to the
North Pole**

Wind and water hazards

Peary's main party followed the trail made
by Bartlett and Borup. When they reached
the first camp they were able to use the
igloos that had been lived in by the two
men. Bartlett and Borup were now only
ten miles (sixteen kilometers) ahead of
them.

On the second day the wind still blew
strongly. As Peary had feared, the wind
was opening up gaps in the ice, where sea-
water flooded in. The party had to wait for
the gaps to freeze again, and they lost a
day. When they set out again, they could
not find the trail. Peary thought that the
drifting ice had carried the trail away.
Later one of the Inuit found the trail, but
he also found footprints of men and dogs
moving south. Borup, who was returning
to Peary for instructions, had missed the
main party.

Lack of fuel

This was serious, because Peary's supply of
cooking fuel had been damaged during
the first day. Warmth from cooking was

▼ Pulling sledges was tiring work for dogs.

vital in such cold conditions, and Peary had meant to tell Borup to bring more fuel from Camp Crane. Peary now sent another team member to follow Borup. Ross Marvin returned to Camp Crane for fuel, while Peary pressed north.

Catching up with Peary

Marvin reached Camp Crane to find Borup waiting. They loaded the two sledges with fuel and set out again, only to be held up by another huge lead. It took five days for this lead to freeze over. Now neither party knew where the other was. Marvin and Borup found a message from Peary in a camp igloo and sent a messenger ahead of them with news that they were on their way. Goodsell, who turned back when his supplies ran out, met the men on his way south. He was able to tell them that Peary was not far ahead. Marvin and Borup had traveled 90 miles (144 kilometers) in four and a half

▲ A dog sledge team in the Arctic today

days. It was so cold that men's breath froze to their faces, and there was a silvery mist from the breath of running dogs — but they had caught up with Peary.

Macmillan turned back next. His supplies were finished and he himself had a frozen heel. Now there were sixteen men, twelve sledges, and 100 dogs left. That day Borup's dogs fell into the water between two blocks of floating ice. He grabbed their traces and pulled them back onto the ice, saving the dogs and 500 pounds (227 kilograms) of vital supplies.

On March 20 Borup's division turned back, and Marvin followed on March 26. The weather was now crisp and sunny, and everyone had to wear ice goggles against the sun's glare. They traveled faster over the smooth ice, but it was still minus 40°F (minus 40°C). By this time, though, the North Pole was less than 180 miles (288 kilometers) away.

▲ Peary searching the horizon with his telescope

The last few days

On March 28 the expedition woke up to the sound of groaning — huge blocks of ice were grinding against each other. As Peary left his igloo, he saw that a wide lead had opened up between his team and Bartlett's. The igloos in Bartlett's part of the camp were slowly drifting on an **ice floe**, toward open water. Peary shouted to Bartlett to be ready to dash across when the floe drifted alongside Peary's floe. There was also a danger of Peary's floe breaking from the main pack ice. Peary and Henson crossed to the main ice with their team, then returned to help Bartlett. At last they were all safely on the main pack ice. After a twenty-four hour wait they were able to continue north.

Nearing the Pole

Four days later Bartlett's supplies ran out, and he turned for home. He left Peary, Henson, and four Inuit with five sledges and forty dogs. The Pole was now about 133 miles (213 kilometers) ahead, and Peary aimed to reach it in five days. During those first few days of April the weather was so good that the team was able to travel more than 20 miles (32 kilometers) each day. Peary took careful sightings of the sun with his sextant as the explorers sped north.

The surface of the ice was smoother and the dogs were able to trot and run. There were few open leads, although the men could hear ice groaning beneath their feet. However, the biting cold grew worse, and even the Inuit began to complain, which they had never done before. Their noses and chins were burned by the biting wind.

▼ Reaching the North Pole was the high point of Matthew Henson's life as an explorer.

"My dream and goal..."

The final leg of the expedition ended at 10 A.M. on April 6, 1909. Henson and the Inuit **tethered** the dogs and began to build igloos. Peary took sightings of the sun. He spent some of that day and the next sledging around to take more measurements. His calculations, which he checked no fewer than 13 times, showed him a position of 90° north. He had reached the North Pole.

Peary wrote afterward, "The prize of three centuries. My dream and goal for twenty years..." In his diary he wrote

▲ The successful team at the North Pole

that the day seemed no different from any other day, and the Pole no different from any other place in the Arctic wilderness! He arranged his team, Henson and the Inuit Ootah, Egingwäh, Ooqueah, and Seegloo around an igloo for a photograph. Each man held a flag, including the Stars and Stripes and the Red Cross flag. This was the photograph of Peary's team at the Pole, which became famous around the world.

The next day, April 7, Peary and his team turned south and began the return journey.

Who was first?

▲ When Peary returned from the North Pole, he was welcomed home by a large crowd.

Peary's team arrived back at Camp Crane, Cape Columbia, on April 23. Once again they had traveled very fast. At times they covered up to 45 miles (72 kilometers) a day. The weather was good — they were not delayed by leads, and there were no gales. They were able to follow their own trail back to land. Peary was grieved to learn that on the way back to Camp Crane Marvin had fallen through the ice and drowned.

At Cape Columbia they built a **cairn** and put a signpost on top, pointing north. The sign read: NORTH POLE, APRIL 6TH, 1909, 413 MILES. While Peary was resting in an igloo, he wrote: "the thing which I believed could be done, and that I could

do, I have done." Then the team left Camp Crane to return to their ship, the *Roosevelt*.

The *Roosevelt* sailed south. On September 6, 1909, Peary and his teams reached Indian Harbor in Labrador. It was from Indian Harbor that Peary sent **cables** to tell the world what he had achieved. He sent one cable to his wife, one to a newspaper, the *New York Times*, one to the Associated Press, and one to the Peary Arctic Club.

A rival claim

Five days before news of Peary's success reached New York, another man had claimed to be the first to reach the North

▲ Cook wearing his Arctic clothes. This photograph was taken at a studio in Brooklyn, New York.

Pole. He was Frederick Cook, an American explorer who had taken part in one of Peary's earlier polar expeditions. Cook now stated that he had reached the Pole almost a year before Peary, on April 21, 1908. Peary was furious when he heard about Cook's claim. He called Cook a liar and a cheat. Cook remarked calmly that he thought that there was room for two at the Pole!

Cook had returned from his polar expedition by way of Scandinavia. He was given great tributes by the Danes. Denmark's Royal Geographical Society and the University of Copenhagen both honored him. Cook then returned to the United States.

Cook arrived in the United States on September 21, 1909. He was welcomed at

a special ceremony to mark his triumph. Peary also arrived on that day, and he, too, was given a glorious welcome. Both explorers were celebrated as the first man to reach the Pole. Yet who was first?

Peary immediately began to try to prove that he was indeed the first to reach the North Pole.

▼ Frederick Cook giving a lecture to the Royal Geographical Society of Denmark. The audience included the king of Denmark.

Peary's triumph

▲ Peary kept detailed notes of his expedition, but Cook could not produce any records.

The **feud** between Peary and Cook continued late into 1909. Cook published an account of his journey to the Pole, but it was full of errors. He had no notes or records of his expedition to show to the authorities. He kept promising to produce his diaries, but they failed to appear. Most importantly, Cook had no scientific information about his journey to show anyone.

Cook vanishes

Then, suddenly, Cook disappeared. There were reports of him from places all around the world — but he was never found. While he was away, his claim to the Pole collapsed. Two seamen, one a sea captain, admitted that Cook had offered to pay them for information about the Pole. He had not paid the men, so now they were

prepared to tell the truth about him. The honors that Cook had been given in Denmark were withdrawn.

However, Cook's supporters were still not willing to agree that Peary was the first to reach the Pole. They began to suggest that Peary's records of his journey were also incorrect. Peary's fight for recognition was not yet over!

Peary proves his case

Cook's supporters claimed that Peary had traveled too fast. They said that no one could have made the journey so quickly in such bad weather conditions. His times were about four times better than those that had been recorded on any other polar expedition. Peary would not give in. He said that a light sledge that was following a trail rather than going over

▲ Cook in Copenhagen, Denmark, talking to newspaper reporters about his expedition

new ground could make very fast time.

Then Peary's photographs were said to be false. Some people argued that the shadows on the photographs were all wrong for the time of the year and the position of the sun. Other experts disagreed and said that the photographs were accurate.

Finally the National Geographic Society held a full inquiry into Peary's claim. They examined Peary's records closely, and they supported his claim. The United States Congress agreed with the society, and Peary was promoted to the rank of admiral. His promotion dated from April 6, 1909, which meant that Peary's claim to be the first to the Pole was officially accepted.

The most honored explorer

In May 1910 Peary received the Gold Medal of England's Royal Geographical Society. He made a tour of triumph in Europe, collecting awards and honors from many countries. Peary was given twenty-two gold medals from geographical societies and three honorary degrees from universities. He was also given the French Legion of Honor. He was the most honored explorer of his time.

▼ Robert Peary and his family in Europe

Every which way to the Pole

▲ Most people use scooters rather than dog sledges in the Arctic today.

After Peary's success in reaching the North Pole, the public seemed to lose interest in Arctic exploration. However, the North Pole remains a place that challenges all kinds of people. Why should this barren place at the top of the world attract so many people? Peary himself probably gave the best answer. He said that the "true explorer" works "not for reward or honor" but because the task is "part of his being."

Since Peary's astonishing achievement, many other people have tried to follow him. They have attempted to reach the North Pole in many different ways — some of them very strange!

Later attempts on the Pole

Peary made his journey by sledge. Other explorers have traveled by balloon, by airship and airplane, by submarine, and on skis. Some people have tried to race to the Pole on sledges or **snowmobiles**. There have been some tragic accidents and some successes, and still people want to be "the first" to the Pole in whatever way they have chosen. They are still following in Peary's footsteps.

By air, land, and sea

An attempt to reach the Pole by balloon in 1897 had ended tragically, but in 1926 an airship was successful. The *Norge*, owned by an Italian, Umberto Nobile, was the first motor-driven balloon to reach the Pole. Flights across the Pole by aircraft were also attempted. Some also failed tragically, but in 1926 Richard E. Byrd of the U.S. Navy flew from Spitsbergen to the

▼ The airship *Norge*

In 1958 two submarines, the USS *Nautilus* and the USS *Skate*, crossed the Pole underwater. These ships were powered by nuclear energy. Then, in 1977, a ship managed to reach the North Pole over the frozen surface of the Arctic Ocean. The Soviet icebreaker *Arktika* cut a way through the pack ice to the Pole and back. The *Arktika* was also a nuclear-powered ship.

Pole and back in fifteen and a half hours. Only one thing went wrong on Byrd's flight. There was a small oil leak from one of the aircraft's engines.

▼ An international party at the North Pole in 1992

In Peary's footsteps

▲ The Peary monument at Cape York, Greenland

In 1986 an international team of one woman, seven men, and 49 dogs attempted to copy Peary's journey. Led by two Americans, Will Steger and Paul Schurke, this team carried all their supplies with them on sledges, as Peary had done. However, they were going only one way. When they arrived at the Pole, they had arranged to be picked up by aircraft for their return journey.

The team hoped to find out whether they could travel as far and as fast as Peary's team. In this way they hoped to prove that Peary's claims were indeed right.

The first woman at the Pole

The expedition set off from Cape Columbia, following Peary's route, and reached the Pole on May 1, 1986. It took them fifty-five days to make the journey. The female member of the team, Ann Bancroft, an American, was the first woman to reach the North Pole. Members of the expedition found that they could make very fast progress over the ice. Steger said later that Peary's speed, which many people thought was too good to be true, was in fact possible. Again Peary was proved right.

Recent attempts

Other expeditions have tried to reach the North Pole on skis. The first solo journey was made by a Frenchman, Jean-Louis Etienne, in 1986. Etienne was helped by regular drops of supplies from an aircraft. He did not have to carry large amounts of supplies.

A Russian icebreaker, the *Sovetskiy Soyuz*, has reached the North Pole on three occasions. The *Sovetskiy Soyuz*, a nuclear-powered vessel, is the world's most powerful and modern icebreaker. It is the only surface ship to have visited the Pole more than once. Its most recent visit was on July 13, 1992, when it carried an international team of researchers from more than ten different countries.

Today, as in Peary's time, there is nothing at the North Pole except ice. Sometimes a country such as the United States or the Commonwealth of Independent States (CIS) sets up a weather station near the Pole. Scientists check on the polar ice drift or gather information about the winds and the weather (meteorological data). Otherwise the landscape is the same as it has been for millions of years. There may be nothing at the North Pole, yet still it attracts people. People still want to go there — and after all, Robert E. Peary proved that it could be done.

▼ The icebreaker *Sovetskiy Soyuz* traveling at about 9 mph (15 kph) through the pack ice on its way to the North Pole.

Glossary

blizzard:	a storm of wind and snow
cable:	a message sent by electricity along wires
cairn:	a pile of stones set up to mark a route or a special place
depot:	a storage place for food or equipment, for use in the future
dog harness:	straps used to fasten a dog, normally made of animal skin
feud:	a quarrel that often goes on for a long time
frostbite:	damage to skin caused by freezing
globe:	an object shaped like a ball that is used as a model of the world
hide:	the skin of an animal
ice ax:	an ax used to dig through ice
ice floe:	a field or sheet of floating ice
igloo:	a shelter shaped like a dome, made from blocks of ice or snow
lead:	a gap in the ice that is wide enough to let a boat or a canoe pass through
merchant:	a person who buys and sells large amounts of goods
meteorite:	a piece of rock or metal from space that falls to the earth's surface
navigator:	a person who sets the route for a ship or an aircraft
pack ice:	the ice that covers the polar area
pemmican:	a Native American food, consisting of blocks of dried beef
search party:	a group of people sent out to try and find a missing person
sextant:	an instrument used to tell one's position by measuring where the sun is in the sky

sledge:	a narrow vehicle with two long strips of wood or metal underneath. In the Arctic they are often pulled by teams of dogs
snowmobile:	a vehicle with an engine, used for traveling across ice and snow
tethered:	fastened to a pole or rock to make sure that an animal does not run away
traces:	straps used to tie an animal to a vehicle
trail:	a path, or route, through the ice and snow
tycoon:	a wealthy and powerful person, in business or in industry
walrus:	a large gray animal with long teeth that lives in the sea

Further Reading

Anderson, Madelyn Klein. *Robert E. Peary and the Fight for the North Pole*. New York: Franklin Watts, 1992.

Herbert, Wally. *Peary, Cook and the Race for the North Pole*. New York: Macmillan, 1989.

Dolan, Sean. *Matthew Henson*. New York: Chelsea House, 1991.

Sandak, Cass R. *Remote Places*. New York: Franklin Watts, 1987.

Steger, Will and Paul Schurke. *North to the Pole*. New York: Random House, 1986.

Stone, Lynn. *The Arctic*. Chicago: Childrens Press, 1985.